# WHERE INCHES SEEM MILES

# WHERE INCHES SEEM MILES

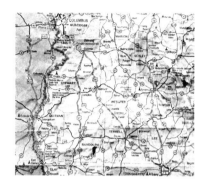

Poems by

## Joel F. Johnson

Antrim House
Simsbury, Connecticut

Library of Congress Control Number: 2013949429

ISBN: 978-1-936482-57-3

Printed & bound by Sheridan Books, Inc.

Book Design by Rennie McQuilkin

Author Photograph by Pierre Chiha

Antrim House
860.217.0023
AntrimHouse@comcast.net
www.AntrimHouseBooks.com
21 Goodrich Road, Simsbury, CT 06070

*To Peggy*

# ACKNOWLEDGEMENTS

Grateful acknowledgement to the editors of the following publications, in which these poems first appeared, some in slightly different forms:

*Blackbird:* "Jèsus and the Snowman"
*The Copperfield Review:* "Another Priceless Audubon"
*Grey Sparrow Journal:* "Her Current Beneath Him," "Where Inches Seem Miles"
*Meeting House:* "Paul and Bennett"
*Rattle:* "Oakbrook Estates"
*A River & Sound Review:* "Its Skin Is Brilliant Red" (as "Snake")

"Eating an Orange, 1348" appeared as part of *Myrrh, Mothwing, Smoke: Erotic Poems* (Tupelo Press)

Several of the poems in the book are part of an online reading sponsored by *Rattle* (http://www.youtube.com/watch?v=rtOXTFK2tQI). You can also see the author read the book's title poem to the accompaniment of a visual diaplay by visiting http://www.youtube.com/watch?v=dCUOiYsMqTE.

Thank you, Joan Houlihan.

# TABLE OF CONTENTS

## I

## II

## III

## IV

# CODA

# WHERE INCHES SEEM MILES

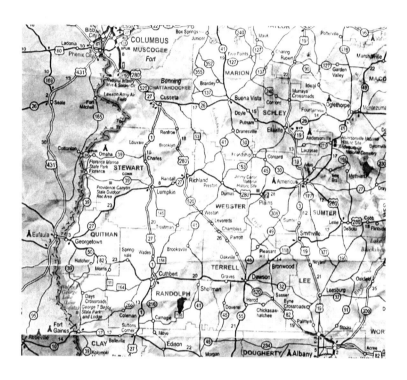

I

# Mamma Said

*This isn't my life. This is someone else's life. I feel so trashy.*

There was no wall of water, no sudden rushing-in,
only a progress the color of mud, flat, indifferent,
spreading across the yard and into the house,
a puddle that grew wide on the kitchen floor then
covered it, absorbing the hall and climbing,
as an old man would, or a toddler, the steps.  And mamma said

*Gardiner.  Do something, Gardiner.  Make it go down.*

We climbed above it, my father speaking almost in a whisper
*Hush, Roselyn, Hush,* his voice trembling but low,
drowned out by the shrieks of Mr. Rickles,
my mother's Pekinese, a dog we hated,
neurotic even on the dullest days and now insane,
yapping in shrill, reverberating squeaks.  And mamma said

*My god, Gardiner, the violin.  We left Phoebe's violin.
You have to go get it, Gardiner.  It's a rental.*

And all the while the dog, the yipping, frantic dog.
I stood at my mother's bedroom window, looked out on a planet
I had never seen, small trees submerged, a lake lapping at rooftops,
cars abandoned to the flood.  And mamma said

*I never wanted to live here.  My people are all hill people.*

Then my father was beside me, raising the window,
the dog struggling in his hands, squeaking and gnashing at him
with its little white teeth.  And mamma said

*Gardiner, Gardiner. My god, Gardiner. What are you doing, Gardiner?*

My father, holding her back with his left arm,
flinging the dog out with his right.
It turned in the air, once, as if between trapezes,
then splashed in the lake of our yard.
We stood there, me, my parents and Phoebe,
dumb as bedroom bureaus, Phoebe's white socks
wet and pink with the dye from her little ballet shoes.
We watched Mr. Rickles swim away.  It began to rain again.

## Riding with Maurice

The day Uncle Linn and Maurice picked us up to ride
in back of his flatbed truck in lawn chairs,
Mom didn't know and Dad came with us.
Linn started slow, the aluminum tubing of the chairs
trembling on the truck-bed as we gathered speed,
then took a few turns, tighter each time, the chairs
sliding and clattering from one side-rail to another
as we screamed, laughed and fought for balance.

Maurice was Maurice Chevalier, Linn's pet crow
that flapped and cawed from a perch welded on top
of the truck cabin.  Speed excited Maurice's intestines
and great white squirts of crow shit came flying back at us,
most of which landed on Lawry's shirt.

When we got to Thrill Hill, Linn gassed it.
As the truck cleared the bump at mid-hill, we went airborne.
Margaret's fanny fell through the chair mesh,
Pete dropped his Coke, and it bounced
over Lawry's head and out the back.
Lawry got a nose bleed or thought he was about to,
and yelled *Daddy, I'm getting another nose bleed!*
but Dad and Linn and Buck Owens were singing *Act Naturally*
and drinking cans of beer from a wet bag on the seat between them.

Maurice had the good sense to leave us on the hill,
flapping off, cawing, indignant, headed home.
Out on the highway, going what must have been sixty
and felt a hundred, Lawry pounded on the cab's back window
but Dad waved him off, threw a beer can up and over Margaret's head,
laughed when she screamed, then shouted back at us,

*Lawry, why do you always have to act like such a sissy?*

Margaret yelled, *Yeah, Lawry. Why are you such a sissy?*
and Pete laughed and hollered *Yeah, Lawry,* but Uncle Linn
slowed the truck down so the chairs stopped sliding and Lawry
slumped in a corner of the truck bed, in the rust and grit.

Mom was waiting in the driveway when we drove up.
Margaret stood before the truck stopped and yelled
*Mama, we rode in back on chairs!* and Mom,
looking not at Margaret, said *I see you did.*

Dad took another sip of his Miller just to show her
it was none of her business if he did, looked past her
to the weedy lawn and broken-down mower he'd left there
and said *Why does your boy always have to be such a sissy?*

Linn unchained the truck gate and said
in that life-long smoker's voice of his, *Y'all come down,*
but Lawry wouldn't budge. He sat there
like he had decided to stay slumped in the back of that truck
until he was old enough to move away. Mom walked around back
and said *You're home, Lawrence. Get. Down. Now.*
But Lawry wouldn't budge for her either.

# A House Buried in Snow

Bennett, small enough to fit,
old enough to go, goes down.
Paul and Louis tie a rope around his waist.
The words rising to his throat,
what he would say but does not.
Knows not to. Not why, but not to.
There's no one here to listen.
He's old enough. Small enough. Goes down.

The chimney air is full of soot.
Small enough, but barely,
down into a tighter darkness,
knees pressed into his chest,
coat back riding up above his head
rope wrenched across his face,
reluctant inches working down
until a foot and then the other, until
his knees and then his gloves find the hearth.

Crawls out and stands, roped and blind,
in what should be familiar but is not,
a cavern so black his eyes cannot distinguish
ceiling from floor, door from wall,
himself from whatever waits beyond his skin.

He unties the rope, kneels on the stone hearth
and lifts his mouth toward the rectangular light above:
those who sent him down. *OK,* he calls.

# Richard Junior

*I have always loved a good ham.*

A gray-bearded man with eyes the color of a lemur's,
flesh not so much exhibiting a farmer's tan as defining it,
neck and forearms dry, cracked, brick-red and brown,
his chest whiter than a porcelain tub, my cousin,
a man who wears a tractor cap, cut-offs and hunting boots to the beach.

*raised on acorns, finished in a peanut field with table scraps.*

His words invested with the slur of south-central Georgia, nothing like
the refined cadence of Savannah or the chain-store dialect I left behind,
no, an argot of its own, the catatonic articulation
of those without the will or strength to lift their upper lips,
the words a flow continuous, each
a backwash of the one before it, oozing into what will come.

*Kill it at first frost. Smoke it with hardwood, hickory if you have it.*

Evoking the smoke shed where his father also hung hams,
a structure tacked together with indifference to the principles
of form, stability and strength, now standing in its seventieth year,
a shed adjacent to the one where Richard and I,
ages six and five respectively, crawled beneath the corn cribs,
snatched the dangling tails of rats and yanked their butts
tight against the wooden slats above our heads.

*Hang it for a year at least, more if you got time.*

This same man, who, for sixty years, has lived
within a radius of ten miles, leaving it a day,
a week at a time, never a month, my mother's sister's son,

alien and familiar, his wife housecat friendly, houseboat big,
lumbering and funny, gracious to her guests from up north.
Invites us to her table where the lazy Susan is set:
corn my cousin grew, potato salad, beans, sweet tea and ham.

# Service for Six, Incomplete

Lovely, isn't it?  I mean in an overwrought sort of way.
This flatware is my share of the family heritage, incomplete.
Some rose of Ireland must have had a pressing need
for butter knives.  Not that Daddy would have cared.
Daddy was always sympathetic to servants of a certain age and figure.

Just a splash, thank-you.

Ridiculous, isn't it? My great grandmother was one of the 400!
She had those high Scandinavian cheekbones,
a long neck and just enough railroad money
to fit the proportions of Mrs. Astor's ballroom.

Our family's dancing days are over, I'm afraid.

She married the source of our profligate gene,
the one Daddy displayed with such panache.
Her son threw himself from a high window in the Woolworth building.
God knows why.  It's what people did in those days.

My grandmother went soon after, influenza or gout,
one of those diseases people don't get anymore.
So there's poor Daddy, twenty-three years old,
all alone in that big house when Mummy sails in.
She liked what she saw,
blue eyes and some nice Orientals.

Turns out Daddy was richer in chattel than cash,
but Mummy made do.  I think they competed
to see who could waste the most.
This is what's left, some knives, some forks,
some mismatched spoons.  A piece of what
Mummy liked to call the ambassadorial china.

## Making One

A Big Mac is hard.
It has a top bun (the #1 bin)
a bottom bun (the #2 bin)
but also
and this is the hard part
because of the layers
a middle bun (the #3 bin).

If you unfreeze too many middle buns
you have too many
and you're supposed to throw them out.
If I have to choose
when the manager is busy
and he says *You choose*
I choose too many.
People don't like to wait
for their buns to unfreeze.

Most everything else is the same.
Two patties, no cheese,
one slice tomato, two pickles,
lettuce not too wet,
secret sauce.
The secret sauce comes in plastic jugs
so even though I work there
I don't know the secret.

Since it's a special meal
not like a cheeseburger
which gets wrapped in paper
(even a double cheeseburger
just gets wrapped in paper)

it gets a box.
At first, I didn't know how
to fold the box so it stood up.
Now I do.

## Where Inches Seem Miles

To slow the approach, one may stop to ask directions,
note the grease engravings on the gas man's finger
as he traces a route on blue highways,
the skin of the map trembling in his hand,
the network of roads connecting like neurons.

This one has been folded too many ways, its edges furred,
holes worn in the four-corner conjunctions,
towns eaten away by hard use until,
driving, one is reminded of what's been left—
a straggle of houses, satellite dishes and half-eaten lawns,
a dog or two, a church or two, another store with little to sell.

Green hatching is a state park,
its picnic tables represented by what appear to be scraps of Sanskrit.
The lake is an irregular clover leaf shaded blue
though its water has been brown always,
its trees draped in moss, the lasting whir of cicadas,
its river a wiggle scribbled by a child.

Roads like veins, paper like flesh, names of towns
written in empty places. But when you get there,
there's always evidence of some man's sweat—
a half-plowed field, a no trespassing sign,
our old house painted a different color, half its trees cut down.
A dog or two, a church or two, enough graves to justify a fence.

## Last Days

His chest is dimpled and tender from all those bullets,
his feet too swollen to fit his red boots.

When the old nurse comes for his massage,
he closes his eyes so not to see the dust mites
in her hair.  Remembers Kansas,
twelve years old flying over the green and yellow fields,
or coming home under a half moon, the spikes of corn
like bristles on a brush.
The nurse finishes,
helps him into his pjs, rolls him out
to an ornamental pond.  He can see
colors we can't—a violet moss edges
the underside of oak bark, rust-colored carp
pull lavender wakes.
He can hear mewing underground,
kit fox cubs in a burrow across the pond.

Superman has never seen his own blood,
can't remember his mother's face, still grieves
for Lois. He's anxious
for the mother fox to come home,
hears his name spoken once
light years away. *Kal-El.*

# Eating an Orange, 1348

First flies then crows then pigs
pulling apart the carcass in front of her cottage.
She can't cross without stepping over
the braids of its intestines.
Tries to remember the orange,
its shallow pores and round weight
warm as a breast in her palm.  He said

*It won't keep.*

Cut it with his knife
juice spreading on her table, a sticky stain,
the white flesh of opened skin, the seeds,
the smell of it, the brilliant juicy chambers—
how they sprayed as he tore them apart with his fingers,
the crushed pulp tart enough to tighten her cheeks.
The color. The taste again. The color and the smell.
When the flies came, he said

*We can't stay.*

The plague came with the flies.  He got sick
then everyone else, her mother, his parents,
the mercer, the potter, the abbot, the smith.
She pinches closed her nose.
Tries to remember the orange.

## Shakespeare's Wife, Anne, After His Death

But I have what your will forgets.  Each page
touched by your pen, word crossed out, every play,
part and line, each direction for the stage,
so much paper to keep or give away,
enough, I think, to fill a man-sized box.
All that buttery sweetness, pots of ink
poured out for made-up love.  How your heart knocked
for any woman but me!  Yes, I think
I'll let you sleep with Portia on your breast.
What would I do with what the great Will wrote?
Best to let you lie with what you loved best,
your comfort when the flesh begins to bloat.
The pages you adored have found their home
and cursed be he who moves my husband's bones.

# Dinner on the Patio

The gas-fired grill is stainless steel,
the chairs Burmese teak.
His oldest was accepted at Yale.
He chairs a foundation
for African women with AIDS.
Assured of his assurances,
industrious, prosperous, something of a wit,
he expects respect and gets it.

I watch his wife watch him talk.
She rests her long fingers
(those long fingers)
at the base of the stem of his glass.
Lifts her chin to catch his words,
a laugh withheld in her elegant throat.
Does she ever think, I think,
ever remember how her long fingers,
how she, how we—Does she
ever remember what I remember?

## Christmas Party

How she rests her fingers on his arm when she speaks to him.
How she says, "Who do *we* know?"
How they leave together, his hand at the small of her back,
the car ride to her apartment.  What comes next I know I know.

I've seen her fingers at the buttons of her blouse,
how her hair falls forward until she lifts her chin,
the scent climbing from beneath her throat.

What I would give not to know, to be
a stranger scanning tickets at the terminal,
a bartender with worries of his own. To not know
how the blue sheet tangled around her leg.  To live
in any flesh but flesh her flesh has known.

## Too Much Room for Words

The palm trees on this card look like rubber,
the sky poured plastic, the beach awfully empty.
Was its sand ever so groomed?
Its waves so evenly spaced?

You said the houses on stilts looked like Martian tripods.
Gone now.
You said we could sit on that porch the rest of our lives.
The way the water looked, you said, would never get old.

I'm sending this to the last address I have for you.
Turn it over.  Believe what you see.
The sky was this blue, the sand this white.
Everything that matters is on the other side.

## Charming Cape, River View

In that house, I learn to grill.
We have dinner together every night, the four of us.
In summer, Julia and I drink wine on the porch,
watch boats drift by, neighbors
out for an evening paddle.
They call up to us and laugh.

In that house, we buy Roger a kayak. He paddles off
to see his friends or they all come to our house
because our house is so lively and so fun.
We put a pool table in the basement
and foosball. They all hang out there and Linda
doesn't leave, because who would ever leave
a house as fun and beautiful as that house?

In that house, I learn to paint.
I get up every morning before the others.
I go out on the porch, the morning light
soft and blurry, ducks out on the river.
I have a cup of coffee in one hand,
a paint brush in the other.
Everyone is happy and asleep,
Roger in his room, Linda in hers.
I'm out on the porch, sunlight filtering through the pines.
God, I hate my house. I hate everything about it.

II

## He Says Her Name Is Venice

She wears a leotard with sequins, which, as she raises
her white arms and twists slightly left, slightly right,
shine.  She is barefoot, on tiptoes, her lifted hands
crooked out like the heads of swans, her hair in tumbling piles.
She stretches out inside his box, toes out one end,
head the other, that hair falling in coils.

The magician's lips are purple as heart meat,
his manicured fingers white as one of his doves.
He takes the saw, toothed and gleaming
from its case, mirror-bright, sets its edge and starts
to cut, steel teeth biting deep in strokes.

I tell my mother I want to leave, but we don't.
Shut my eyes.  The sound of it, the gasping
rake of the blade as it climbs and falls, plunges
and rises, each upstroke an echo of the down,
higher-pitched, squealing and grunting
as it makes its way through her.

## How It's Done

Find a member of the opposite sex let's say female
a female you find attractive for reasons having nothing
to do with anything that will ever come out of her mouth
and look at her not the way your mother says you should
but in that other way and having looked
feign interest in what interests her
her fluffy kitty her mom the paintings of Thomas Kinkaid
the novels of Nicholas Sparks whatever she decides
against her better judgment to confide once you've given her
two Cosmopolitans and the sympathetic look you learned
watching the Lifetime channel and if you can deliver that look
land it with just the right blend
of boyish charm and manly understanding
or what after some vodka and cranberry juice
she'll glom onto as understanding
she'll tear-up not weeping which is a waste
and a very long evening but a near-weep which
she would describe as this sudden feeling
of being like-you-know *connected*
and you would describe as a half-decent chance
bought for a couple of pink drinks
a deal to get done when she drops her eyes your cue
to reach across and touch not her hair not her cheek just her hand
and barely that just brushing the knuckles as if even that
short faint warm soft touch is more than you would dare
so it's her move not yours when she takes your hand
looks up into the eyes of a man she can finally trust
who like-you-know truly *understands* her
and like-you-know really *knows* her
and after you have as the saying goes known her treat yourself
to a Starbucks either the mint or mocha frappuccino
choose mint plunge the straw deep as it will go
and take that first cold swallow.

## Midnight at Gray's Papaya

It was raining when I crossed Broadway,
the kind of rain that falls heaviest on the inside,
so I ducked in here,
a place where only strangers get a table.

I'm not immune to Sinatra,
to moonlight and memory, the pit-pat of droplets on dogwood,
but it all washes away like yesterday's *Post* in an East River drain.

Every broken heart between 85th and 57th finds her way here.
They like to rinse their tears in french fries and daiquiris,
but it's the loneliest room in New York, a graveyard for the soul.
They're infected with romance, crave candlelight, but come to Gray's.
This is chrome and linoleum.  Extra fluorescent.

I find a stool at the counter.  Order a hot dog.
There's an off-duty receptionist two stools down,
not half-bad.  I don't say anything to her
and she says nothing back at me.
I can tell she'd respond to the right type,
a guy who likes dogs with big floppy ears.
Forget it.  I come here for the cuisine.

## Are You Safe at Home?

We're required by law to ask.
Some don't understand, ask me to explain.
Some (the men) make a joke.
Once, a Laceration said
*Yes, thanks to this!* Pulled out a pistol
right there in the emergency room as if
anyone in an emergency room would see
anything funny about a drunk with a handgun.

When a Contusions comes in alone,
you see the sunglasses at night, the tissue
for the eye that won't stop tearing,
how she walks like the floor is ice,
and you already know, so you try
the gentlest tone you can muster,
your kindest, nicest, sweetest voice, saying
*Honey, are you safe at home?*

You're praying for a no,
down on your knees begging
for that one word *no*
so you can call social services,
get her, for once in her miserable life,
help, half a chance to get out, but
before you've even finished asking,

you know.  Before you ask, you know.
So when she nods her head, those sunglasses
hiding her eyes, you're already there,
desperate for her chance, pleading

*Honey, you have to say it out loud and if*
*nodding your head means no, just say it,*
*just say no and we can get you some help, honey.*

She turns away, blue tissue wet and wadded
in her fist, lips trembling, and you allow yourself to think
for once, just once, you may have done some good
but then she says *yes* and you say *Are you sure?*
and she says *yes* again and you remind yourself
you're a nurse, just a nurse, so you say
*Tell me about your accident.*

# Theodore F. Baldwyn Retires

My pitcher cat is plump, pours from her right paw.
Invaluable at breakfast, she was useless after lunch
until I invented the cat martini.

*A little pussy before dinner?* I'd inquire.
My wife, as dull as she was old,
as fat as she was dull,
never really liked that joke.
Never liked any joke of mine.

But she did enjoy her cat martinis.
They were my last attempt (fruitless, I'm afraid)
to put a bit of meow back in the old gal.
I'd watch her wallow to the dinner table,
two pussies to the wind,
consider ways to be rid of her.

Our dinners were dreary recitations of the faults
of one Theodore F. Baldwyn, inventor of the cat martini.
The theme: he made little to invest and lost what he invested.

*Still enough for one, my dear. Just enough for one.*

I assured her it was a splash of Tabasco, *for friskiness.*
That was a year ago this March.
Dinners are quiet now, each day routine,
a couple of kit-nips in the afternoon, a howling tom at bedtime.

## To My Daughter Going Out

I cannot watch you leave this house tarted up like a teen harlot
without at least suggesting, my innocent,
that nothing's to be gained from bringing fresh fish to old cats.

The most effective chaperone is a girl's own ethics.

I will, therefore, activate the GPS on your cherry-colored phone,
monitor every mile, block and inch
that ill-mannered, unwashed, tattooed vulgarian drives you.
You will call me, my dear, letting me know
where you are, what you're doing, with whom and why
every quarter hour if not more.

I need not remind you what happens when a girl is not particular.
Your half-sister Suzy does that all too well.
I expect you to offer these low-riding shag-haired sloths
nothing more than a stone-cold liking.
I'm watching you, Margaret.  Have fun.

## Antigonus' Lament

I do as I am told, keep the infant alive long enough to die
on a bare rock at wood's edge where weasels will find it,
mice, crows and squirrels, creatures that nibble and peck,
where the sun will blister its eyes, gnats swarm its nose,
ants fill the winding tunnels of its ears.  Hers.

Her eyes.  Her nose.  Her ears.  Nursed her
with goats' milk, cleaned her, kept her dry and warm
though the voyage was blustery and wet.
She could have been our own, the girl we lost
when my wife still was young, still could bear
the sight of me, a courtier in ascent, promising and promised,
eager to prove my salt's worth to the Sovereign.  Proof.

This is proof.  She's sleeping as I lay her down.  Cries when I turn
to leave.  I go back, stand so my shadow falls across her face.
It calms her.  I step aside.  The sun stabs her eyes.  She cries again.
I lean over her. Even this is comfort.  Nearness.  Semblance of caring.

## Dinner with the Hand Models

Those cuticles!  Bart, dear, when was the last time you had a
  really deep manicure?

      Let me guess, how about never?
      Would never be about right, Bart?
      Look closely, Rachael.  Those are the hams
      of a man who doesn't give a damn!

I'm sorry, Bart.  Stephen can be so crude sometimes.
Of course you care.
It's the occasion, I know, casual dinner, old friends.
Were we not so casual
you never would have come with nails like those.

      Oh, for Christ sakes, Rachael! As if a few minutes
      with an emery board would mean anything to those sausages!
      Let me guess, Bart,
      if you're popping out for an errand on a cold day,
      you know, a quick biff with one of your little tarts,
      you don't even wear gloves, do you?

Now who's being ridiculous?
I'm sorry, Bart.  Stephen can be so vulgar.

      Vulgar?  You want vulgar?
      Take a look at those knuckles, Rachael.

Stephen, our guest did not come here
to have you insult his knuckles!
I'm so sorry, Bart.

Yes, Bart.  Rachael is sorry.
Rachael is just a little sack of sorriness
whenever you bring your greasy nails around.
But, Rachey-poo, wasn't it you
who started in on his cuticles?
Maybe if you had more confidence in your own
you wouldn't be criticizing his!

What?  My cuticles?  *My* cuticles?  I can't believe it!
Even on a night when all we are trying to do
is have a casual dinner with an old, old, old friend
you must return to the subject of my cuticles!

I am simply saying...

You are simply saying what?
I'm sorry, Bart.  Ever since that spread in *Vogue,*
you know the one—"Have hands that say *Caress me!*"

Caress my ass!

... Stephen has been beside himself with jealousy.

Jealous!  Of what?  Those paws?

Yes, jealous!
You be the judge, Bart.  You're objective.
Would you say that my hands are ... caressable?

I've seen cows with softer hooves than those meat hooks!

Vulgar, crude and jealous!

Squid with cuter tentacles!

I haven't seen your hands in *Vogue,* have I?
They wouldn't flop those scaly old fins in *Motor Trend*!
Really, Stephen, I'd gladly scratch your eyes out.

Then why not do so, darling?

The stress, sweetheart.  My nails simply couldn't bear it.

## You Ask If I Am Happy

I have watched an eclipse cross a street puddle
fierce and diminishing in unexpected twilight.
Seen birds rise behind stained glass,
their shadows redeeming the lifeless plates.

If happiness is bright scraps,
vivid rags torn from a succession of days,
I would answer as a wino would
rolling a basket with busted wheels,
growling at the climbing of birds,
the progress of the moon.

Is this happiness?  A schizophrenic with a shopping cart,
all wet tatters, broom handles, hub caps and cans?
I'm as happy as that.
Happy in a way that is inexplicable and random.
Predictably, routinely and unavoidably sad.

I am fifty-four years old and as unprepared
to find, collect or keep happiness as I was at age twelve.
You ask if I am happy.  Yes.  I'm not.

III

## Oakbrook Estates

When the mayor, who is black (our second),
reviewed the subdivision plans, he asked
about lighting, curbing and lot size, about square footage
and average price before he asked, as if in passing,
*What about the old oak, will it have to go?*—and I,
older than the mayor, old enough to remember its name,
knew which oak, and said possibly not, we could keep it
for green space, and the mayor, walking me to his door,
said it would be good to have green space, this pleasant
chocolate-skinned man never acknowledging
the oak's name, though from his question,
from the carefully casual way he asked, I think he knew it,
had been told the name by a father or grandfather
though neither could have seen it, as I did, or been there,
as I was, when last it was put to that purpose,
and I, the lesson's last witness, then a boy of seven or eight
watched how the feet turned, twisting first left then right
then left again in car light, the head obscured, dark
above the beam, though I strained to see it, wanting
to see how the neck looked, how the rope looked,
the dead face, trusting as a boy of seven or eight will trust,
that it was just, that my elders had taught a necessary lesson,
but wondering if it might have been more
just to have selected someone older, since this one
seemed in my eyes, in a boy's eyes, watching
the body twist in The Lesson Tree,
in the stark light of Buford Neil's station wagon,
too small, too young, almost still a child.

## In the Glossary of Rights

You know what he says to me? He says
*Can my daughter use your facilities?*
Can you believe that?
His *daughter*. My *facilities*.
Like she is Eleanor Roosevelt
and my gas station is the Taj Mahal.

So I say, being polite, because I believe
you try to be polite no matter who it is,
*No, I'm sorry. It's whites only.*
But he just stands there and I can see
he too is trying to be polite, and I
respect that in a person
no matter how dark the tan.

He says, *But she has to go.*
She's about six or seven, cute as
a chocolate drop, her hair tied up in pink scraps,
one pigtail heading north, the other due west.
I say to him, *You know what would happen
to my business if I started letting Negroes
use my rest room?*

And he says (cool as a cucumber)
*Probably it would pick up.*
Swear to God. That's all he said.
*Probably it would pick up.*

And that is the day I sold my soul to the devil,
Martin Luther King and the N double-A CP.
That dirty little toilet in back of my gas station

became the first integrated *facility* in Crisp County, Georgia.
And you know what? Business did pick up.
For every white customer I lost, five coloreds
came in to buy peanuts, Co-colas and Juicy Fruit.
My *facilities*. Don't you just love it?
Where you reckon he learned that word?

## Pimento Cheese

At Christmas, mamma got sentimental,
crying in the pimento cheese.  She said
*It's what gives it the bite.*  That's my mental
picture: she's either cooking or in bed.
She would read or sleep or just look outside,
waiting for birds at an empty feeder.
She gave me the job one Christmas to ride
with Daddy to colored town with cedar
wreathes and cheese sandwiches for those in need.
*The tears give 'em the bite,* I'd say.  But they
never got it, their faces pinched with fear
when the door opened, then acting so pleased.
Daddy stayed in the car "out of my way"
and smoked, his eye on the rear-view mirror.

## Jèsus and the Snowman

It's a west Texas thing:
three Delco car batteries strapped to a switch lighting a line of icicles.
Draped from barbed wire.

As far north or south as a man can walk in a night,
a clutter of jackrabbit holes and arroyos,
cactus and yucca,
sand too coarse to be good,
too dry to be dirt.

A plastic snowman guards the south end of the illuminated line.
Cheerful in its green tie and top hat, its buttons and broom, carrot nose.
Ridiculously round.
The balls of its head and chest light up the sage
like St. Elmo's fire.

Decoration for the chiggers and toads, fire ants and lizards.
For the ones who cross at night,
taught by word of mouth to know it as a beacon,
a place to meet at 3 a.m.
where, after fanning out for 10 miles or more,
they can regroup, drink some water, fan out again.

It's 5 a.m. when Jèsus finds the snowman.
It should be cold, but it's warm.
He huddles against it, stone-eyed and afraid,
trying to look past the snowman's lasso of light.

There are three figures moving toward him,
silhouettes in wide brimmed hats against a pale horizon.
Hearing them before he sees, knowing he will want to be erect,
Jèsus stands, tries to button up a smile.

## Megan Flanagan

I dress to match her dining room drapes,
speak softly loud enough for her to hear,
know when to knock on a downstairs door.

I keep my cuffs and collars spotless.  When she bathes,
I sponge her back, flesh dimpled and pink at the folds.
Wheel her to the study, wait as she reads.

I think I can hear her think.  *Mam,* I say.
*The fire,* she says.  Coal in the grate balanced
in fragile cliffs, crimson-seamed and brilliant.

# Another Priceless Audubon

*"After Audubon rendered the birds, Mason painted the background."*
from *Discovering the Unknown Landscape*


That snipe enters from the right, her shanks yellow garlands,
her white breast stealing the eye from bog gloom beyond.
The gloom is mine.  It fills (I measured) three-fifths the canvas
but none see how crowded light catches
in the understory of the oaks, how Spanish moss frames the sky,
trapping in its wig damps from the mire.

I think of the swamp I braved for him,
our boat beneath a drapery of snakes,
the air fetid, fever-imbued.  Sedge entombed in gas.
A place named for Dismas, crucified with Christ.
Dismal, to play the supporting part even in the final hour.
I craved a yellow ague just to breathe
my last on dry, untrembling ground.

And Audubon all the while:
*Observe this, George.  Observe that, George.*
Mr. Mason to you, sir.

What I observed was a sun struggling in baldcypress,
learned from it frugality with light, to keep only what's needed
to suggest a wood beyond the painter's reach,
a wildness held in leash.

## Getting Late

I love you guys.

      Excuse me?

You mean more to me than
my own brother, my own father, my own wife, man.

      Your wife?

I mean it, guys.  When I think about us growing up,
sneaking out to skate, air so cold the snot froze in your nose,
Carl riding that snowmobile in his reindeer underwear,
Ralph putting that sturgeon down Bruce's pants. I think
without you guys, without those times,
I wouldn't even be here.

      You're right, Lee.  Without us, you'd be sober, home,
      and in bed with your wife.  You're welcome.

No, I'm serious, guys.  This is something I need to say.
I mean, I hope we'll be doing this shit years from now –

      You mean drinking, Lee?
      I think you can count on that.

- but you never know.  One of us could be killed in a car crash,
spin out and end up hanging from some tree, all mangled and stuff,
and I never would have told you how I feel.

      I feel like another beer.

One of us could have cancer, one of those kinds
you don't feel until it's all in your blood, in your

stomach and your liver and I just don't want that to happen
without saying what you guys mean to me.

Lee? Would you do me a favor? Please shut up.

You know what? I want us to all hold hands, just for this minute,
this one minute while the four of us are here together,
none of us sick or dying or already gone, no wives around or kids.
I just want to hold your hands so I can say I love you.

Jesus, Lee. Shut up.

## Generous Friend

I have known inside your silver box
seen what gifts you are being owed as a children
of the children of the father of Kenyatta.
That is why I choose to conclude you
because you are an outstanding foreigner
and your box is hanging on
where others have leaves so many years ago.

Please send Mastercard.

As Secretary for the Pretty Nice Inheritances,
it is my duty to see inside what is green
like a gambling table.  There are many royal things
for you and for your children laughing with his hands.
I smell a rock in it the river with baby's breath beside it,
find the feather of a purple bird, the bloods of many wives.
I see all the things I do not say.

Please send Visa.

I have paid the Freighted Forward because
it is my duty for finding and because, foreigner,
I have seen without your eyes the royal gifts for you.
When I open it first and feel the felt
I see and see for you.  Now I know and wait your call.

Please send Discover.

Oh, outstanding foreigner, generous friend,
your box is hanging on where others were safes but not so good.
None now but yours with hinges like the fingers of a girl.
I think what song I hear but then it is your hinges
and I have known inside, the feather and the smell.

# Rattled

He hardly had cause to cut my head off.

>We was quail hunting.  I stopped to take
>a whiz and soon as I got going, he got going.
>Sounded like the whole world was rattling,
>up front, out back, everywhere.
>Trees, brush, bush, rattling, rattling, rattling.

To be perfectly frank, he frightened me.
I had slipped out onto a favorite stone
to enjoy some sun.  It was so delicious
I must have dozed off.  I woke up
with him standing practically on top of me.
That awful smell they have was everywhere.
He was urinating, of course.  Aren't they always?

>So there I am,
>some dumb fuck with my dick in my hands
>and I'm thinking this is it, boy.
>I'm gonna get bit and it's gonna be six weeks
>before they find my sorry ass back in these briars.

Of course I rattled.  Who wouldn't?
At a moment like that, it's all instinct.

>It's like I was on automatic pilot,
>looking around with nothing but my eyes
>trying to figure out where he was.

He was enormous, six feet or more,
seeming all the taller for standing so close.
I simply wanted him to see me and move away.

Finally it occurs to me
to stop looking around and look down.
Jesus, he was huge, six feet three inches
coiled up on a rock right by my leg.

Did he strike? Did I strike? It was all so fast.
I experienced a pain so swift, so specific
as to be almost erotic.

Thank god I'd brought that old machete from the truck.
One minute it's rattling, the next it's flopping around with no head.

It must have been gruesome looking,
but what I recall most vividly...

I remember standing there in that honeysuckle bawling my eyes out,
thinking there'd never be another day like that one.

... is this ethereal sensation of tranquility,
an almost visceral conviction (ironic, I know)
that there would be other days, other warm rocks in the sun.

# In the Bullet Room

I'll thank you to put that back.
Not all history is public, you know.
That ball was pulled from Hamilton's breast.
Do you have any idea how reckless it was to shoot Hamilton?
No, I don't think you do . . . What?
Of course we keep them! What would you have us do,
let the bloody surgeons auction them off?
I think not.
It is appropriate that they be kept and kept private.

I can't tell you how ghastly this room was when I first came here,
little pedestals and private shrines.
I chucked it all when I found this cabinet.
It's from the old card catalog room at Library of Congress.
I like the democratic feel of same-sized drawers.
Kennedy, Garfield, McKinley, each has its own coffin,
four by two by nine, the labels hand lettered.

Of course, someone always wants to "make improvements."
Reagan insisted on writing us a note
when his slug was added to the collection.
The joke about "forgetting to duck."
I shipped it off to Archives, p.d.q.

*Let the bullets speak for themselves,* that's what I say.
Want to know why the Viet Nam war dragged on?
Consult the drawer labeled Kennedy, R.F.
Want to help your fellow man? See King, M.L.

Can you what? I suppose ...
but only if you promise to go soon.
I'm very busy you know.

Go ahead, open it.  Kennedy, J.F.

Ha!  You were expecting an extra bullet, weren't you?

Well you might as well open that other one.
I know you won't leave until you do.
Lincoln, A.
Be my guest.
But be prepared for disappointment.
It is so very small.

## Say-Say Mobley

Never got remarried after her husband,
Little Bobby Ross, got burned up by the Japanese.
He was sent home from Guadalcanal
in a government-issue steel casket
with a sign on it that said *Do Not Open.*
She did, of course. Say-Say was a stubborn somebody.
Her mama (Sarah Mobley Senior—we called her Lu-Lu,
same as we call Say-Say Say-Say, not Little Sarah)
said *Child, don't you open that box.*
Begged her not to, got down on her knees and pleaded with her,
but Say-Say was one to do what Say-Say wanted.
She pulled that lid up, and what-do-you-think—
there was nothing in there but a dog tag,
a piece of helmet about the size of a butter plate,
two hands and a pile of ash.
Lu-Lu must have sat up every night for the next six months
with a cold compress packed on top of Say-Say's head,
every light in that house turned up just as high as it would go.

## Beside the Backhoed Earth

Spare me the folded flag, the white gloves,
your re-worked sermon and brown gaze.

Send me a mother, one to match me
boy for boy, loss for loss.  Let us
talk girlfriends, caskets and favorite songs,
compare the measure of children's graves.  Let her
climb with me into this one, defy the world to make us leave.

Show me what she keeps in her cardboard box:
the pinewood derby car, the trophy,
the bottle of sand from Venice Beach.  Or the picture
beside the TV set, the uniform and crew cut,
the closed door upstairs.  No, send me a mother,

not a speech, not a flag, not a cause or a reason,
no personal note or comforting call.
Send me someone who knows how to suffer,
who grieves as I grieve and cannot sleep.

## Swing Set

Here most people sleep, windows open, doors unlocked.
What guns they have are stashed in closets.
What knives left in kitchen drawers.
What keeps a few awake is problems that never hurt a soul.

Here, you could live for eighty years,
choose lettuce from the pile,
fetch the dry-cleaned sport coat,
walk for health, stop to watch the girls swing,
how their shorts billow as they rise.
Wish that it was late enough to drink.

But I'm not fit for playgrounds.
Raised in twenty houses, left twenty schools.
What was my drinking arm ends just below the elbow.
Flesh raw from Agent Orange, I talk small,
but I have been a reason not to sleep.
Held my lighter to the roof of a hut and let the gooks weep.
Came at night to round up the men.  Returned for a couple of girls.
I watch the swings. Say less than what I think.

## In the Glow of Time and Violence

It was 1913.  I was not yet engaged, soon to be widowed.
Evelyn Loris and I shared a cabin, portside out.
We coaled at Suez, elegants in tinted glasses and picture hats
steaming along a shore of dun-colored hills, sand fantastically white.

After the War, every hour of that trip would seem its last.
The attitudes and fashions, the feckless cheer
of those young men with nothing to do, evaporated.
Once lost, the light that bathed our little boat
and discovered the crests of minor waves
found a new immensity.

But I remember how it was.

Dull.  Fateless.  Vacant sky and languid days.
I think of Teddy Banard in his spotted waistcoat
pretending to look through binoculars.
A martyr now, blown to glory at Marne,
but Teddy, alive, was such a silly man—
all those trivial hours with no premonition of their conclusion.

## Postcard

I need a new planet, a place
where winds of boiled ammonia blow,
where a man, cresting what was unclimbed,
looks from a lava dome, sees for the first time,
as only a first man can,
mottled slime, canyons carved in sulfur,
multitudes of lizards trickling scales of lust and pearl,
where leather raptors fill the air
whistling spherical hymns of praise
for moons that drop one by one by one,
shavings from the maker's plane
curling, falling, shedding light.

IV

## Eating Japanese

We slip off our shoes, eat sitting on the floor,
miso soup and tempura at a table two feet tall.
Chop sticks. I'm clueless, barely 20. She says, *No, like this.*
Folds her hands around mine. Seeds an obsession
that has lasted me forty years. Even the blouse she wore,
an Indian tunic, embroidered white cotton, how
those sleeves slid back from the bones of her wrists.

I was a virgin in sock feet, face flushed, breath short,
her slender hands on mine.

No regrets. How can anyone say that?
For me, no matter how good life is,
the wife, the kids, the house, the job,
it will always be that other life, the one I lived without her.

# Her Current Beneath Him

She pours her hands across his eyes.
The delta of her hair spread out around her upturned face
flows under him
away from him—
what he would have but cannot keep,
 a current continuous, leaving.

Falls with him from high ground,
from forests and drumlins
through mill towns and bluffs,
through cut crops and steep fields,
ryegrass, hayweed and thistle,
past wolf trees, barns and feeding horses.
They fall and rise
and fall again,
fall to where he cannot swim or see or breathe,
the water cool and newly made. And he

will never find his way back,
will put his fingers to his lips
and wonder that they ever touched her.

## Its Skin Is Brilliant Red

Her eyes withhold what has been mine.
Her shoulder raised to shield her cheek
as a bird hides in the crook of its wing.
The contours of her back, indentations of her spine,
my own rib fastened there,
her hair, her calves and curving wrists
still soft from their creation.
All this and everything within me
an argument for tasting it.

## On Fucking Cammie Parker

Words fail.  Take *gratitude* for instance.
When Cammie began to unbutton her blouse
to describe that feeling as gratitude
that sonorous tolling of desire
that murmur of lava, tremble of earth
that sudden, scarlet rushing-up thundering
in my head, my heart, my—

Well.  You get the point.  Or *pulchritude.*
To reduce to the Latinate the pendulous sway
of her pink-tipped breasts, the bell-like sweep
of waist and hips, the lavish tangle of her hair
the bowl of her ribs
giving way to the clinched dash of her navel
and below that—

Well.  I think you understand the *plentitude*
of pleasures that briefest of hours brought to me
the ecstasies of flesh and tongue
synapses sparking, sinews pulsing
the heaving up and plunging down
the little nibbles, licks and sighs, the—

Well.  You can imagine the *beatitude*
I felt, Cammie's round shoulders in my hands
the ridges of her throat beneath my lips
her white teeth grinding in my ear
her nails raking down my ribs
her hungry—

No.  I think you will agree, the English language
such as it is, fails.

It can't capture
the gratitude and pulchritude
the beatitude and plentitude
of fucking Cammie Parker.

## Metropolitan

A businessman in boxer shorts leans against the wall.
It's early, a hotel room in Midtown.  He woke

to the sound of her, rhythmic, vocal, urgent on the other side,
rousing him from half-sleep.  A night of horns and back-up warnings
then this, her, a voice wordless through the wall.  He lies

beneath synthetic sheets, waiting for an end that won't come,
creeps across the room, now stands, a blind voyeur, his ear
pressed to sheetrock, not yet thinking what he will think:
A prostitute.  Faking it.  Giving her client what he pays to hear.

Thoughts to be thought over coffee and buns
in the morning meeting at ten.  Not yet,
not in this empty room, inches away, so close,
without this wall, he could reach across and touch her.

# Marketing to Men

She smiles at me. *Free pictures of women,* the web ad says,
as if they were not everywhere and free, these pictures of women,
women on glossy stock and cheap pulp, billboards and bus signs,
women hung on every wall of every gallery
of every East-end, South-side, oak floor, white-walled walk-up,
women in tilted frames on every inherited bedroom bureau.
Books burst with pictures of women.
Women on paper cups and three-ring binders,
silk-screened on t-shirts, backpacks and shopping bags,
little videos in taxis and elevators, on laminated cards in airplane seats,
women smiling, pouting, posing.

Rain is more rare than pictures of women.
I've seen fewer dogs than pictures of women.
For every car ever built, there are ten million pictures of women.
Shy or bold, staring down the camera, half mostly hair,
a few with no hair at all.  Still, we can tell

they're women.  Pictures of women
clothed and unclothed, active and inert,
laughing, drinking, sleeping, talking, smoking,
taking it off, putting it on, holding it up,
standing in it, standing on it, chopping it, mowing it, mulching it.
See how they cook and shop and squeeze and choose,
how they mold, mash, crush, crunch and cream it.

In black and white and color, in 3-D, painted, drawn and photographed.
On the bottom of every grain of sand, a picture of a woman.
On the back of every star, a picture of a woman.
Every atom, particle and neutrino, a picture of a woman.
It's what gives the universe weight.  And still
I'm tempted.

## She Likes Her Luckies

She takes a long drag, her eyes puckered shut
the string purse of her lips cinched tight
cheeks brown and dry as a paper bag.
        Hacks and hocks her coffee-colored phlegm.
            Regards it on the ground.

*I like to smoke*, she says.

Me, I like to lie in bed with a cigarette.
Read the catalogues.

I like the way it feels in my lungs
how a fresh pack smells and the way
smoke moves along the ceiling
        like a leaving tide.
          I like the way
it fills out the screen in old movies
floating beside Ingrid Bergman's hair
like some idea she's having
        but is afraid to say.
I like the way
    ash grows long
        nothing holding it together
          but what was just there.
I like a silver lighter in a lady's hand
    how the cowboy's nail can scratch a match.

When my husband Robert was alive
we had a smoke vocabulary.
Blowing it out your nose in short bursts to show
you were amused.
    A way of looking up,
        opening your mouth,

letting the cloud rise from it—
the thought of what's been said.
A long stream blown out hard to say
you have had just about enough.
Tilting the head back
taking it down deep in the lungs and sinuses
prelude to sex.


Victoria's Secret.  J Jill.
It hardly matters as long as
there's a cigarette.
You see those models?
Those thin legs?
Those skinny arms?
They smoke.

The President smokes.  Of course he does.
After they've all left—
the Secretary of State
the Secretary of Defense
the Assistant Chief of Staff.
Alone in the Oval Office
dark now, dark at last and finally quiet.
The orange coal of his cigarette.

I've never had a bad one
not one I wish I hadn't smoked.
More likely, I put one out and think:
I wish I had another.
I'm no more addicted than a word to its meaning.
Saying you're addicted makes it sound like
you don't want one.
But I do.
I want every one.
Every one I can get.

## Paul and Bennett

And Paul.  Taking the quiet oars, the quiet
thump of the oars, glides, with a single
stroke that interrupts the water's sleep,
already piercing the fog, dissolving
into its soft canvas, a shape subsumed
into its own shadow.  And Bennett

waving in comic slow motion,
half turned in the back of the boat,
knees toward Paul, his face toward their mother,
calling goodbye as if a mile away,
though but a single stroke, now two,
fading deeper into the vague canvas,
shades subsumed, merging.  And she

standing on the damp cold wood of the dock,
feeling the rotted ribs of its grain beneath
her bare feet, wants to laugh but cannot,
would wave but does not do that either,
watching the pierced fog heal, the interrupted
water return to its waiting dream, finds
regret out of all proportion to their leaving.  Sees

Bennett's face turn away, a pale dial,
turning toward Paul and the smooth
deliberate roll of his shoulders, pulling
back on the oars, another stroke,
and beyond, the indefinite cloud
that is gathering them in, concealing them,
Paul and Bennett, shades merging,
more shape than substance now, fading.  Hears

Bennett's quiet voice, the sound of it only,
the words indistinct behind the vague canvas,
and in reply, a low laugh, Paul's,
coming before and after the rhythm of the oars,
words that, lacking form, carry all meaning
in their tone, in the way they cross the water,
leaving definition and syntax behind,
returning to stillness.  Their sound

dissolving on the canvas before her,
subsumed, Paul and Bennett,
falling into a gathering cloud,
a dream as it slips the conscious mind
more real for being half forgot,
all that she would keep but cannot.

## At Home, the Backyard in August

I'm always sleepy and never just sleep,
dreamed last night I was with my mother
though I haven't seen her face in fifty years.
She was wearing her wool car coat, her hands
on the wheel of Dad's old Buick.
She looked at me, about to speak,
more real than any part of this world she's left me in.

I see the other ancients at the park,
how they gaze up at the bones of trees and
trace the paths of sparrows from walk to branch to sky.
Dad got this way. I'd stash him in the garden
with a tumbler of vodka and a bowl of Cheez-Its.
He would look at the peaches on the table in the sun,
smell the grass and weep.

## Visiting Saint Anselm's

*Will you get in bed with me?*
Not what one expects.  Not since five or six
have I been that close to his lung-rise.

Then, his chest was tight as a football,
ribbing sturdy as a boat's.  Now
the flesh is milk blue, his lungs close to closing.

Where the shoulder knots, a bedsore.
Of course, it is necessary to do this thing, this right thing,
a tender story to tell the wife.

But what if a nurse walks in?
Shoes off, ridiculous in sock feet, I lift the sheet,
check for body leaks.  Climb in.

His johnny is tangled, coming undone,
his cheeks bristled and collapsed.  Once bright as pins,
his eyes drown in a viscous jell.

I can smell his breath, the pillow, his bedsore.
He is a withered elf.  The bones
of his hands touch the ripening flesh

of mine.  I remember my boy at five or six
snuggled against my ribs, a creature of my own making,
mysterious and loving.  It was a lark to have him there.

This is no lark. My father's eyes are open horrors.
Eggs of spit at the corners of his mouth.
I should have been his daughter.

A woman would know how to do this thing.
Comfort the flesh.  Deal with the eyes.
What if a doctor walks in?

His bones and my bones.  An uncertain breathing
climbs up my nose.  He clings to my hand.
The creature of his making, I try to let him look.

## Having It

We keep a drawer for keys in case
we find the locks they fit.  I found
his glasses there, his tie clip in a box of nails,
an old coat next to mine,
sleeves slightly bent.
I think of the way he signed his name,
the looping *C,* the staggered *H*, the wild wiggle that followed,
his thin hair and thick hands, how his sneezing shook the house,
how, once, he came out to watch me
shoot baskets, sat in a folding chair,
drank his can of Miller and said
*Today I have it all.*

# CODA

## Notes from an Undelivered Lecture

—but now, with April fast unfurling,
the swallow's egg beneath the eaves,
it's time we scale those steeps again,
ask more of limb and will than what the frost has left us.
Every sunrise rinsed in brine summons the aboriginal,
ignites the heart, heats the brain.
The burgeoning lilacs, the progress of squalls,
the pitched lilt of the dove's return beckon us
to a busier world, there to decipher
the hieroglyphics of the bee,
the print of hoof and paw across the pliant earth,
the paths bats paint on twilight's dusky canvas.
A green chord vibrates within us.
Each impatient day reveals its eager branch,
flooding veins of limb and leaf with hues of eastern yellow.
Who would waste, thick-lidded and slow, when
fox and vole, trout and fly, finch, worm, hawk and hare
scramble, splash and plunge?
Surely these eyes were not forged to trace the drift
of slash and vowel across the drowsing page?
These sinews and thighs, were they coiled to rust unused?
Let us—

# ABOUT THE AUTHOR

Joel F. Johnson grew up in Georgia and lives in Concord, Massachusetts. He participates in workshops at the Concord Poetry Center, where a raucous gang of friends and poets has read, critiqued and improved nearly every poem in this book. Joel is a self-employed businessman with a wife and three children. These four intelligent, funny, loving individuals are the center of his life.

This book is set in Garamond Premier Pro, which had its genesis in 1988 when type-designer Robert Slimbach visited the Plantin-Moretus Museum in Antwerp, Belgium, to study its collection of Claude Garamond's metal punches and typefaces. During the mid-fifteen hundreds, Garamond—a Parisian punch-cutter—produced a refined array of book types that combined an unprecedented degree of balance and elegance, for centuries standing as the pinnacle of beauty and practicality in type-founding. Slimbach has created an entirely new interpretation based on Garamond's designs and on compatible italics cut by Robert Granjon, Garamond's contemporary.

To order additional copies of this book
or other Antrim House titles, contact the publisher at

Antrim House
21 Goodrich Rd., Simsbury, CT 06070
860.217.0023, AntrimHouse@comcast.net
or the house website (www.AntrimHouseBooks.com).

•

On the house website
in addition to information on books
you will find sample poems, upcoming events,
and a "seminar room" featuring supplemental biography,
notes, images, poems, reviews, and
writing suggestions.